# Forests in the Clouds

Melinda Laidlaw
and Julie Nickerson

**Forests in the Clouds**

Text: Melinda Laidlaw and Julie Nickerson
Publishers: Tania Mazzeo and Eliza Webb
Series consultant: Amanda Sutera
Hands on Heads Consulting
Editor: Jarrah Moore
Project editor: Annabel Smith
Designer: Leigh Ashforth
Project designer: Danielle Maccarone
Illustrations: Dan Crisp
Permissions researchers: Helen Mammides and Lumina Datamatics
Production controller: Renee Tome

**Acknowledgements**
We would like to thank the following for permission to reproduce copyright material:

Front cover: iStock.com/Cede Prudente; back cover, p. 21: Minden Pictures/Alamy Stock Photo; p. 1, 23 (bottom): crbellette/Shutterstock.com; p. 5: iStock.com/TT; p. 6: Vera NewSib/Adobe Stock; p. 9 (top): Nigel Hicks/Alamy Stock Photo, (bottom): Gerry Ellis/Minden Pictures/Nature in Stock; p. 10: Peter Cripps/Alamy Stock Photo; p. 11 (top left): David_Khelashvili/Shutterstock.com, (top right): 24K-Production/Shutterstock, (bottom): DedMityay/Alamy Stock Photo; p. 12: Stephen Dalton/naturepl.com; p. 13 (top): Vital Hil/Shutterstock.com, (bottom): iStock.com/Toa55; p. 14: Robin Weaver/Alamy Stock Photo; p. 15: Andrew Merry/Getty Images; pp. 16, 17: © Queensland Museum, Gary Cranitch; p. 18 (top): blickwinkel/Alamy Stock Photo, (bottom): iStock.com/JanelleLugge; p. 20: Monika Gregussova/Shutterstock.com; p. 22: Ondrej Prosicky/Shutterstock.com; p. 23 (top): Martin Pelanek/Shutterstock.com; p. 24 (top): Colin Anderson Productions pty ltd/Getty Images, (bottom): pipat wongsawang/Getty Images; p. 25: Minden Pictures/Alamy Stock Photo; p. 26: Ingo Oeland/Alamy Stock Photo; p. 27: Graham Crouch/Newspix; p. 28: dmitry_islentev/Shutterstock.com; p. 29: Karina Bostanika/Shutterstock.com; p. 30 (top): Minden Pictures/Alamy Stock Photo, (bottom): iStock.com/Milan Krasula.

Every effort has been made to trace and acknowledge copyright. However, if any infringement has occurred, the publishers tender their apologies and invite the copyright holders to contact them.

NovaStar



ISBN 978 0 17 033464 8

**Cengage Learning Australia**
Level 5, 80 Dorcas Street
Southbank VIC 3006 Australia
Phone: 1300 790 853
Email: aust.nelsonprimary@cengage.com

For learning solutions, visit **cengage.com.au**

Printed in China by 1010 Printing International Ltd
1 2 3 4 5 6 7 29 28 27 26 25

*Nelson acknowledges the Traditional Owners and Custodians of the lands of all First Nations Peoples. We pay respect to Elders past and present, and extend that respect to all First Nations Peoples today.*

# Contents

# Cloud Forests

A cloud forest is a very special type of rainforest. Cloud forests are found at the tops of some high mountains in **tropical** and **subtropical** areas, at heights of between 900 metres and 2500 metres. They are called cloud forests because they are often blanketed in low clouds, even down to the forest floor.

As they are found on the tops of mountains, cloud forests are usually small. They make up only 1 per cent of the world's forest areas, but they collect a large amount of water that then flows into creeks and rivers. They are also home to many plants and animals that do not exist anywhere else in the world.

Cloud forests are found in many countries, including Costa Rica, Mexico, Peru, Ethiopia, Papua New Guinea and Australia. Some well-known cloud forests are in the Gondwana Rainforests of Australia and in Monteverde in Costa Rica.

## Cloud Forests Around the World

This map shows some of the world's best-known cloud forests.

Like other rainforests, cloud forests grow in places with very high rainfall. The wet ground is covered in a layer of fallen leaves called "leaf litter". The **canopy** is very **dense**, so the forest below receives little sunlight. This keeps the cloud forest cool and moist. Because of the low levels of sunlight in cloud forests, plants grow slowly.

The Monteverde Cloud Forest in Costa Rica is the biggest cloud forest in the world.

# Water in the Clouds

## The Water Cycle

The survival of cloud forests depends on clouds forming through the water cycle. In this cycle, light from the Sun hits the surface of the ocean, and the seawater warms. As it becomes warmer, the seawater changes from a liquid into a gas called "water **vapour**". This process is known as "**evaporation**".

As the water vapour rises higher into the **atmosphere**, the vapour cools down and **condensation** occurs. Condensation is when the water vapour changes from a gas back into a liquid, in the form of millions of tiny water droplets. These water droplets are so light that they float in the air and form clouds.

Clouds form over the ocean.

As the number of water droplets increases, the clouds become heavier, and the water falls back to the ground as rain or snow. This is called "**precipitation**". Water then flows through creeks and rivers, back to the ocean, and then the cycle repeats.

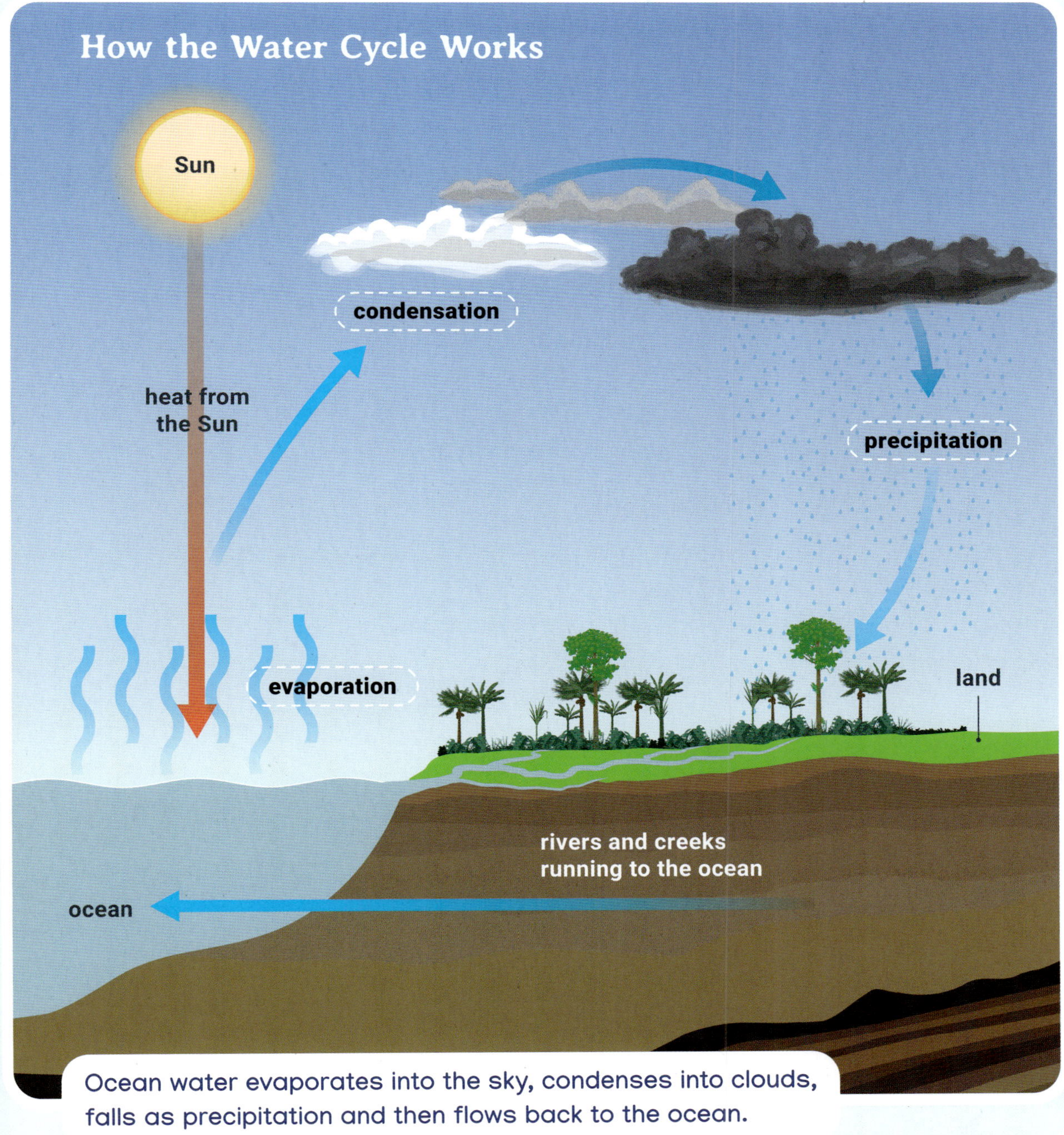


Ocean water evaporates into the sky, condenses into clouds, falls as precipitation and then flows back to the ocean.

# Using Cloud Water

When water vapour rises towards a cloud forest on a mountaintop, it cools down and forms clouds. In a cloud forest, this condensation happens among the trees, because they grow so high on the mountain. The water droplets in the clouds collect on the leafy canopy and drip to the forest floor below. This "cloud drip" can provide over one-third of the cloud forest's water every year.

Cloud forests, and the plants and animals that make these forests their home, need this cloud water to survive, especially during the drier months of the year and in times of **drought**.

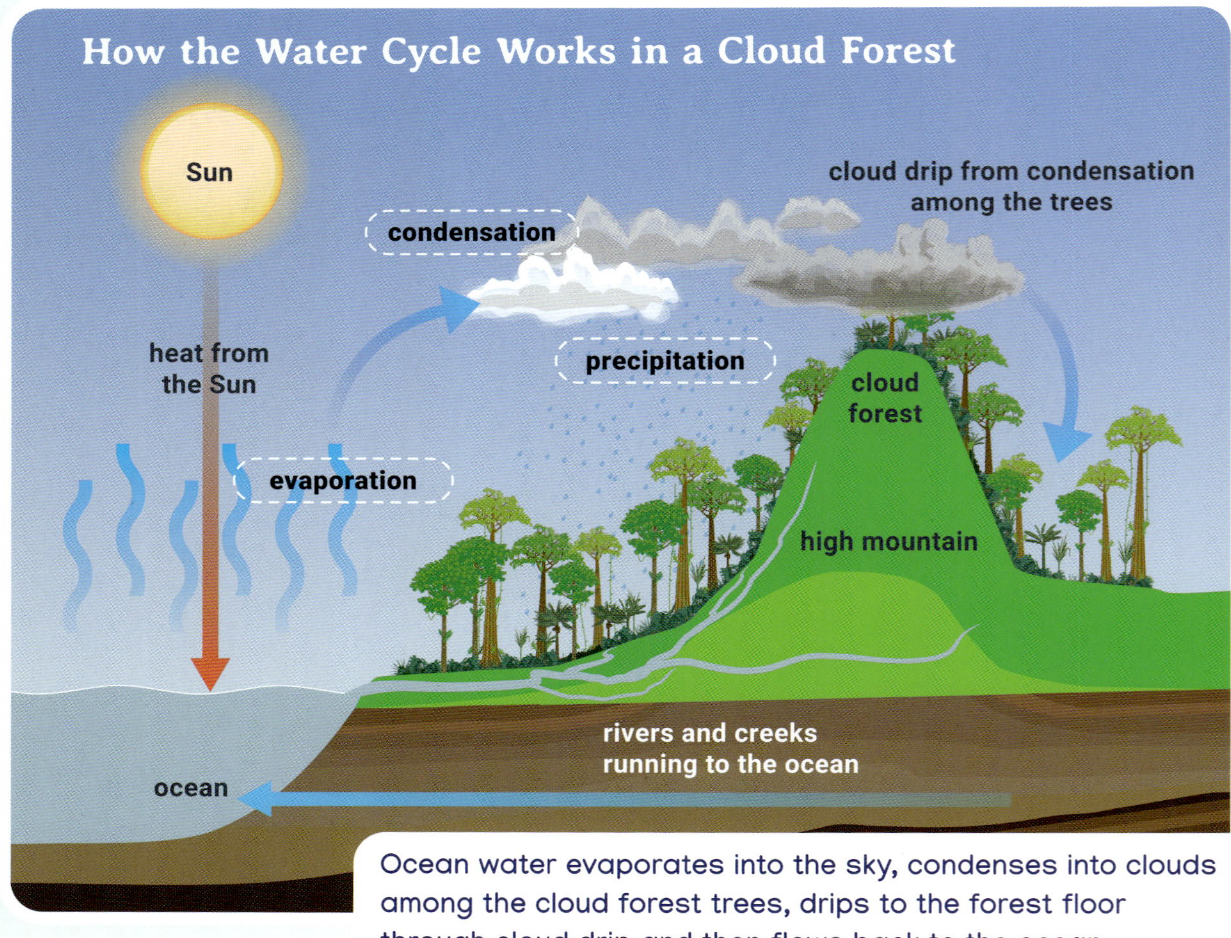


Ocean water evaporates into the sky, condenses into clouds among the cloud forest trees, drips to the forest floor through cloud drip and then flows back to the ocean.

Cloud water drips from the canopy to the plants underneath in a cloud forest.

## Drip Tips

The leaves of many cloud forest plants have a “drip tip”. This is a pointed end that allows water to run quickly off the leaf and onto the forest floor below.

# Habitats and Climate Change

The habitats of animals and plants in cloud forests are affected by changes in **climate**. Earth's climate has been changing over many millions of years. Some changes are due to natural causes such as the release of gases from volcanic eruptions.

But many other recent climate changes are the result of human activity. For example, the burning of **fossil fuels** such as coal and oil produces large amounts of **greenhouse gases**. These gases trap heat inside Earth's atmosphere, causing the temperature of the planet to rise.

Coal power stations produce greenhouse gases, contributing to climate change.

These rising temperatures can make events such as floods, droughts and bushfires more severe. The extreme conditions during these events can cause changes to habitats. When a habitat changes, it affects the chances of survival of the animals and plants that live there.

Water rushes through a river during a flood.

A riverbed dries out and cracks during a drought.

A bushfire rages through a forest.

# Cloud Forests and the Climate

## *Drier Habitats*

Cloud forest habitats can be affected by warmer temperatures caused by climate change. In warmer temperatures, water vapour has to rise higher to cool down enough for clouds to form. In the future, this may mean that cloud forests at lower **elevations** get less water from cloud drip. If that happens, the habitats in these forests will become drier.

When plants do not receive enough water, they can **wilt** and die. Animals may be forced to move to higher ground in search of moist, cool environments. As they move higher up the mountain, their habitat area will become smaller.

Hummingbirds live in the Monteverde Cloud Forest in Costa Rica.

## Bushfires

With their wet environments, cloud forests are usually not at risk from bushfires. However, climate change has increased the chance of bushfires in countries like Australia and the USA. Hotter, drier conditions and less rainfall in many areas increase the bushfire risk. When plants have wilted or died, they may burn more easily, helping the fire to spread.

In dry weather, plants can wilt and turn brown.

Bushfires burn more easily when a forest is dry.

# Surviving in a Drier Habitat

As cloud forest habitats become drier, the plants and animals that live there will need to **adapt** to survive the changing conditions. Some will need to move to a new habitat or find a way to survive in warmer environments with less water.

Fruit bats live in the Gondwana Rainforests in Australia.

The cloud forests of Gondwana in Australia and Monteverde in Costa Rica are two places that are home to rare or endangered plants and animals whose habitats are being affected by climate change.

# Cloud Forests of Gondwana

The Gondwana Rainforests of Australia extend from south-east Queensland into the middle of New South Wales. The cloud forests in this area are home to many native plants and animals, including some that are endangered. These plants and animals will be increasingly affected if their habitat becomes drier.

Between late 2019 and early 2020, fires burned more than half of the Gondwana Rainforests of Australia. These destructive fires are known as the Black Summer bushfires. The damage to the Gondwana Rainforests was due to low rainfall and many years of drought. Even some cloud forest areas burned in these fires, showing how dry the plants and habitat had become.

The Black Summer bushfires burned more fiercely because the forests were dry, including the cloud forest areas.

# Black-tailed Antechinus

The black-tailed antechinus (pronounced *ant-uh-kye-nuss*) is a small marsupial that lives on the floor of the Gondwana cloud forests. It feeds on tiny animals and insects such as millipedes, spiders and maggots, which it finds among wet leaf litter.

The black-tailed antechinus is an endangered species.

The black-tailed antechinus was named as a new species in 2014. However, its numbers are decreasing and it is already endangered. This is because its habitat is becoming drier and because of predators such as foxes.

Scientists are finding some black-tailed antechinuses at higher elevations. This suggests that they can move higher up the mountains, where there is more food and water. This behaviour will increase their chance of survival.

This rare antechinus was named for its distinctive dark tail.

Fortunately, the cloud forest habitat of the black-tailed antechinus was not badly burned in the Black Summer bushfires. But the increased risk of bushfires due to climate change is still a threat to these animals, and they may face extinction in the future.

## Tiny Bear

The scientific name for the black-tailed antechinus is *Antechinus arktos*. "Arktos" is the ancient Greek word for "bear". While the black-tailed antechinus is only 20 centimetres long, it was given this name because it sometimes stands up on its back legs, like a bear!

# Antarctic Beech Tree

One tree species that relies on the moist cloud forest of the Gondwana Rainforests is the ancient Antarctic beech tree. These trees have grown in Australia for millions of years. They are currently only found in a few areas of high elevation with plenty of rainfall along Australia's east coast, including the cloud forests of the Gondwana Rainforests. Some of these trees are many thousands of years old.

Antarctic beech tree in the Gondwana Rainforests

Antarctic beech trees can have huge roots that look like tangled knots.

Antarctic beech trees have wide, knotted trunks, and their canopies can reach as high as 50 metres into the air. These dense canopies provide a large surface for cloud water to drip to the forest floor. This increases the amount of water for the roots of the Antarctic beech trees and for the other plants and animals that share their habitat.

Clouds reach the tall, wide canopies of Antarctic beech trees, allowing cloud drip to fall to the forest floor below.

The tangled roots of the Antarctic beech tree help to support it during strong winds. They also provide many holes and spaces for animals to hide or hunt for food in. Leaf litter collects in these spaces and, as it breaks down, it provides the tree with nutrients.

## Freezing Fossils

The Antarctic beech tree doesn't grow in Antarctica, but fossils of ancient beech trees have been found there. Scientists believe the trees grew in Antarctica long ago, when it wasn't as cold there as it is today.

Case Study 2

# Monteverde Cloud Forest

The Monteverde Cloud Forest is located in Costa Rica, a country in Central America. The forest is home to a wide range of animals, from small insects to jaguars and pumas. Due to climate change, the Monteverde Cloud Forest is experiencing longer seasons of drought, making this habitat drier.

Monteverde is nearly always covered in cloud.

# Golden Toad

The golden toad was first discovered in 1966 and, unfortunately, is now extinct. It lived only in the Monteverde Cloud Forest. Scientists believe it is the first animal in the world to have become extinct as a result of climate change.

There are a number of reasons why this may have happened. The golden toad lived underground in cool, wet conditions. It required puddles of water for its eggs and for the growth of tadpoles. The hotter, drier conditions changed the golden toad's habitat, and this may be what caused it to become extinct.

The golden toad was also affected by a **fungus** called "chytrid" (pronounced *kye-trid)*. This fungus is found in wet environments worldwide and causes a skin condition that kills animals such as frogs and toads. It may spread into cloud forests more easily as climate change causes temperatures to rise.

Golden toads were named for their bright golden colour.

# Resplendent Quetzal

The resplendent quetzal is a bird found in the Monteverde Cloud Forest. It is also found in southern Mexico and other Central American countries.

The cloud forest habitat of the resplendent quetzal is changing due to rising temperatures. Unlike the black-tailed antechinus, the Antarctic beech tree and the extinct golden toad, this bird can move quickly and fly to other mountain areas in search of food, water and shelter. Its ability to live in different places increases its chances of survival.

A male resplendent quetzal takes flight.

However, the number of resplendent quetzals is decreasing. In addition to the effects of climate change, some of their forest habitat has been cut down, and the land used for growing crops or grazing cattle.

Female resplendent quetzals have shorter tail feathers than the males, and grey bellies.

## Splendidly Bright

The word "resplendent" means very bright, colourful and beautiful. The resplendent quetzal has bright green, blue and red feathers. The males have magnificent long green tail feathers and bright red bellies.

# Protection of Cloud Forests

## Scientists at Work

To protect cloud forests and the animals and plants that live there, scientists study changes in the cloud forests. They also study the climate, including rainfall and temperature. They use this information to predict what each cloud forest might look like in 10, 30 or even 50 years' time. Understanding how the forests may change in the future is important for the **conservation** of cloud forests and the wildlife that lives there.

Scientists collect data about the birds and animals living in cloud forests.

Scientists collect water in the forest to test for pollution.

# Conservation Dogs

Scientists also study the number, location and condition of plants and animals in the cloud forests. Specially trained conservation dogs are sometimes used to help scientists find signs of animals such as the black-tailed antechinus. A dog can quickly and easily move through dense, wet, steep habitats that may be difficult for humans. Each dog is trained to recognise the smell of an animal's "scat", or droppings. It then searches over a wide area, busily sniffing the ground and plants. When it smells scat, the dog stops and sits. This lets scientists know that the animal they are searching for may have recently visited the area. Scientists can then focus their research on the current habitat of the animal they are studying.

A conservation dog searches for animal scat.

# Laws to Protect Cloud Forests

When plant and animal habitats such as cloud forests are in danger, laws can be made to protect them. National parks are a type of natural area protected by law. These parks have rules that protect them from being cleared for houses or farms. The animals and plants that live there are safe from being destroyed or removed.

Many cloud forest areas worldwide are protected. For example, the cloud forest habitat of the resplendent quetzal in Costa Rica has been made into a national park. This will help the survival of this bird species.

Another way to protect habitats like cloud forests is through making them a **World Heritage site**. World Heritage sites have strict laws about how they are used. This is important for the conservation of important places worldwide. The Gondwana Rainforests of Australia and the cloud forests within them have been a World Heritage site since 1994.

Clouds lie in the valleys of the Gondwana Rainforests.

# Working Together

Discoveries in science are the result of many people working together. This is called "collaboration". To study cloud forests, scientists work with rangers, students, volunteers and First Nations **Traditional Owners** and other scientists. They share the results of their research by giving talks, writing articles and books, and teaching others. Their work helps governments and international organisations protect the future of special places like cloud forests and the plants and animals living there.

Traditional Owners share their knowledge to help protect forest habitats.

# Special Habitats

Cloud forests are special rainforest habitats found on mountaintops at very high elevations, where clouds often pass through them. They are home to many rare and endangered plants and animals. Unfortunately, cloud forest habitats are changing as a result of climate change and land clearing. Scientists are working together to understand these changes and to save and protect these areas.

Many creeks flow from cloud forests to the ocean.

# Working in the Clouds: Field Diary of Dr Rhonda

## Day 1 – Studying the Cloud Forest

*Today, the rangers led me and my team of other **ecologists** into the Gondwana cloud forest. We had stayed halfway up the mountain at the ranger's station overnight. It became colder as we hiked higher up the mountain and into the clouds.*

*For almost 20 years, we have been measuring how the trees grow, die and are replaced in the cloud forest. The rangers helped us find the trees that we tagged on previous visits. We measured the **circumference** of the trees with a measuring tape. We then tagged and identified any new trees that had grown since our last visit to the cloud forest. Some of the trees were growing very slowly, and we estimated that they are many hundreds of years old.*

*One of the Antarctic beech trees had blown over in a storm, leaving a gap in the forest canopy. The sunlight could now reach the seedlings on the forest floor. These seedlings will grow tall and replace the fallen tree, providing habitat for cloud forest animals.*

| **Location:** *Cloud Forest 1* | | | | | |
|---|---|---|---|---|---|
| **Tag Number** | **Circumference (cm)** | | | | **Species** |
| | **2006** | **2011** | **2016** | **2021** | |
| *Tree 1092* | *27.9* | *29.5* | *32.8* | *35.2* | *grey possumwood* |
| *Tree 1094* | *81.6* | *82.7* | *84.4* | *dead* | *Antarctic beech* |
| *Tree 1096* | *326.7* | *459.9* | *471.2* | *483.3* | *Antarctic beech* |

## Day 2 – Conservation Dog

Today was an exciting day. We left the ranger's station early, with our conservation dog, Bella, to work in the cloud forest. Bella is trained to smell the scat of the endangered black-tailed antechinus. We put on her red jacket and **GPS tracker**, then she got to work. After hours of sniffing logs and tree trunks, Bella finally sat down at the base of an Antarctic beech tree, showing us that she had found antechinus scat! Bella was rewarded with a game with her favourite toy, her little ball. Her discovery was proof that the antechinuses were still surviving in this cloud forest.

Bella hard at work

Next, we set up a camera near the base of the Antarctic beech tree. This camera automatically takes photos if an animal moves in front of it. We left the camera in the cloud forest. We will return in a few weeks. Hopefully, the camera will have taken a photo of the antechinus that Bella tracked.

our trusty camera

We were pleased to see the plants and animals in the cloud forest are surviving after the bushfires, but we will need to continue to study this changing habitat.

# Glossary

| | |
|---|---|
| **adapt** (*verb*) | to become used to something, such as weather patterns |
| **atmosphere** (*noun*) | the layer of gases around Earth, including air |
| **canopy** (*noun*) | the upper layer of tree branches in a forest |
| **circumference** (*noun*) | the distance around a circular shape such as a tree trunk |
| **climate** (*noun*) | weather patterns throughout the year |
| **condensation** (*noun*) | the process of a gas, like water vapour, changing into a liquid, like water |
| **conservation** (*noun*) | protection of wildlife and the environment |
| **dense** (*adjective*) | thick and tightly packed |
| **drought** (*noun*) | a period when there is little or no rain |
| **ecologists** (*noun*) | people who study living things and their habitats |
| **elevations** (*noun*) | different heights |
| **evaporation** (*noun*) | the process of a liquid changing into a gas |
| **fossil fuels** (*noun*) | fuels, such as coal, oil and petrol, which are made from dead plants and animals buried millions of years ago |
| **fungus** (*noun*) | a plant-like living thing |
| **GPS tracker** (*noun*) | a device that tracks exactly where something is, using satellites |
| **greenhouse gases** (*noun*) | the gases that contribute to climate change, especially carbon dioxide and methane |
| **precipitation** (*noun*) | rain, hail or snow |
| **Traditional Owners** (*proper noun*) | First Nations people who have lived on and cared for the land for a long time |
| **tropical** and **subtropical** (*adjectives*) | either within the region called the "tropics" near the equator (tropical), or just outside that region (subtropical); tropical and subtropical areas are hot |
| **vapour** (*noun*) | very small drops of liquid floating in the air |
| **wilt** (*verb*) | to droop towards the ground because of heat or lack of water |
| **World Heritage site** (*noun*) | a place of great importance that is given special protection |

# Index